Learning Cursive in Narnia

Cursive Handwriting
for Narnians

Part One: Alphabet and Letter Practice
Part Two: Word Practice
Part Three: Quote Copywork

This book belongs to:

_____

Suggested Use and Schedule

Part 1: Alphabet and Letter Practice

- Learn one letter a day. Demonstrate and show your child how to write each letter, following the arrows.
- First trace over every letter, then copy onto blank rows. The last tracing and copy rows focus on joining the letters without lifting your pencil
- Check your child's work after first line for correct penmanship and to correct any bad habits or confusion.
- Have your child circle their best letter on the workbook page to help train their eyes as well as their hand.

Part 2: Word Practice

- Copy two to three pages a week.
- First trace over every letter, then copy words onto blank rows.
- Check your child's work to correct any bad habits or confusion.
- Have your child circle their best word on the workbook page to help train their eyes as well as their hand.

Part 3: Quote Copywork

- Copy one to three quotes a week, depending on your child's ability.
- The quotes get longer and progressively harder, so depending on your child's pace, they may need to take a few days to finish the longer quote. Keep it fun!
- Check your child's work to correct any bad habits or confusion.
- For a fun challenge, try to find the quotes and read the context around it.

Cursive Alphabet

Part One: Letter Practice

- Learn one letter a day. Demonstrate and show your child how to write each letter, following the arrows with your finger. Emphasize _showing_ technique rather than the telling.

- First trace over every letter, then copy onto blank rows. The last copy rows focus on joining the letters without lifting your pencil

- Check your child's work after first line for correct penmanship and to correct any bad habits or confusion.

- Have your child circle their best letter on the workbook page to help train their eyes as well as their hand.

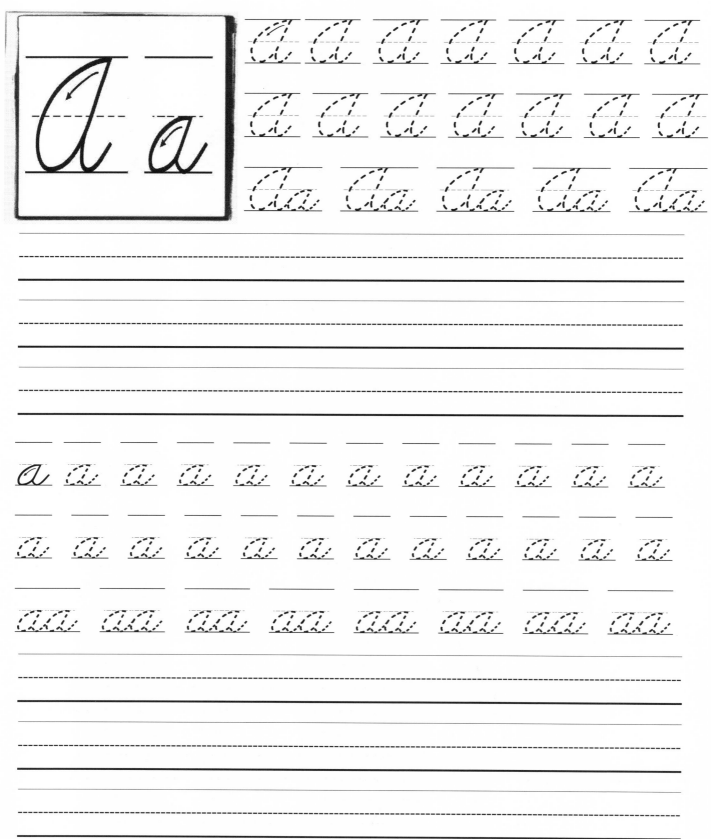

Circle your best letter

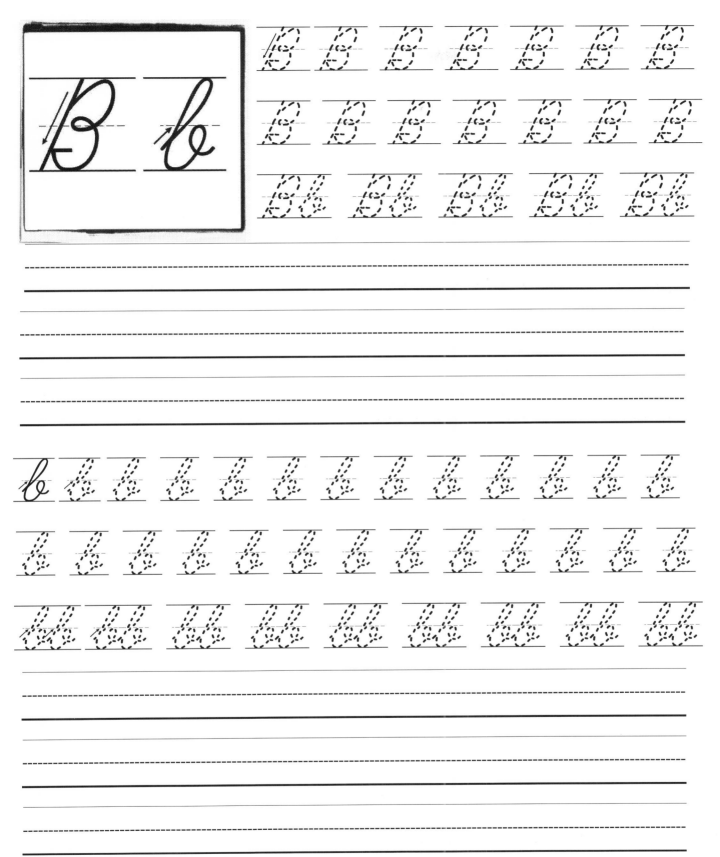

Circle your best letter

Circle your best letter

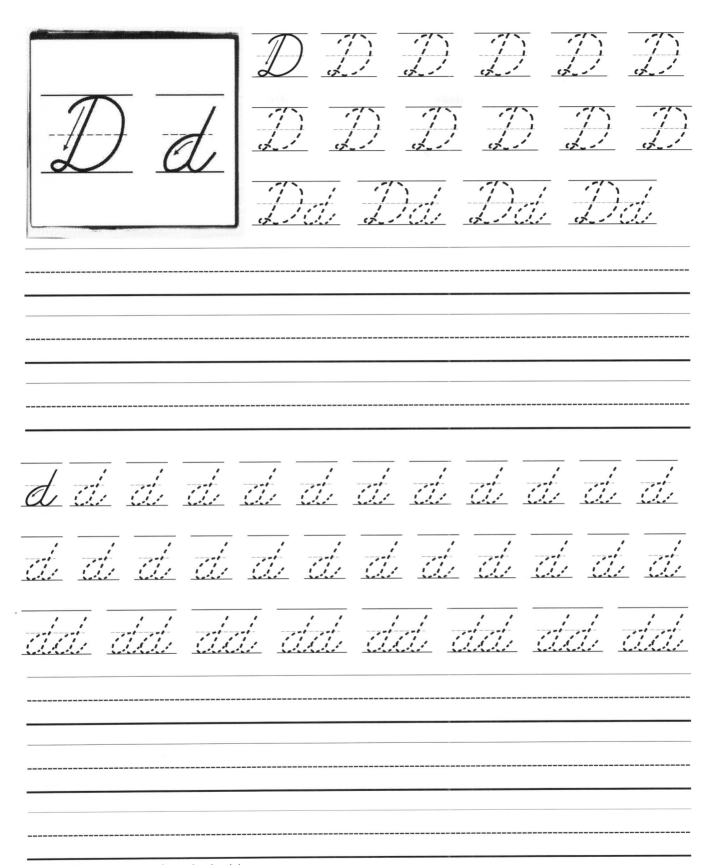

Circle your best letter

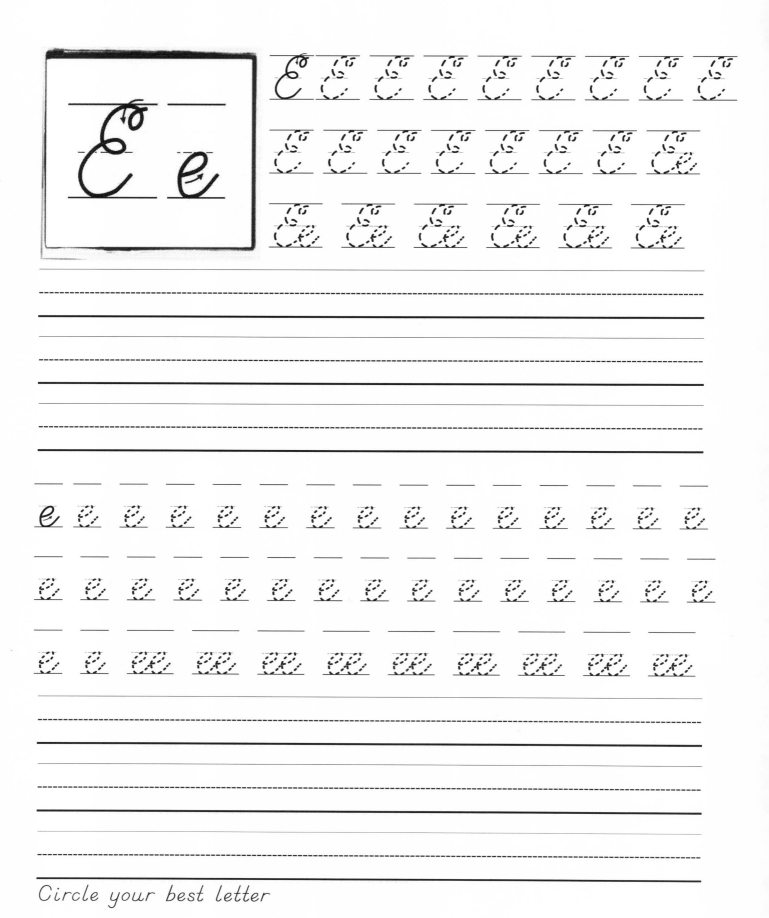

Circle your best letter

$\mathscr{F}\ \mathscr{F}\ \mathscr{F}\ \mathscr{F}\ \mathscr{F}\ \mathscr{F}\ \mathscr{F}$

$\mathscr{F}\ \mathscr{F}\ \mathscr{F}\ \mathscr{F}\ \mathscr{F}\ \mathscr{F}\ \mathscr{F}$

$\mathscr{F}\!\mathscr{f}\ \mathscr{F}\!\mathscr{f}\ \mathscr{F}\!\mathscr{f}\ \mathscr{F}\!\mathscr{f}\ \mathscr{F}\!\mathscr{f}$

$f\ f\ f\ f\ f\ f\ f\ f\ f\ f\ f\ f\ f\ f\ f\ f\ f\ f$

$f\ f\ f\ f\ f\ f\ f\ f\ f\ f\ f\ f\ f\ f\ f\ f\ f\ f$

$ff\ ff\ ff\ ff\ ff\ ff\ ff\ ff\ ff\ ff\ ff\ ff\ ff\ ff$

Circle your best letter

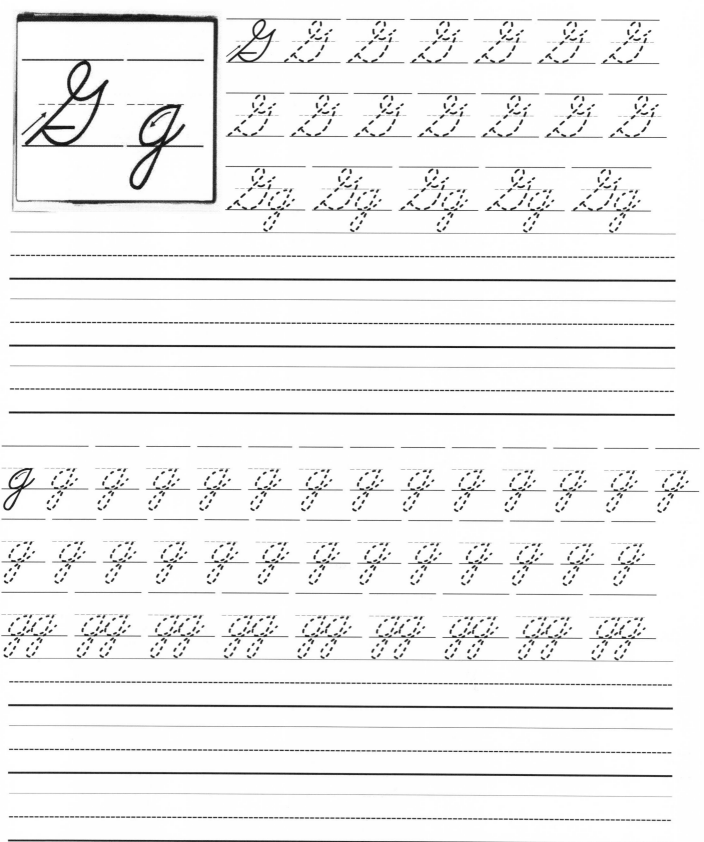

Circle your best letter

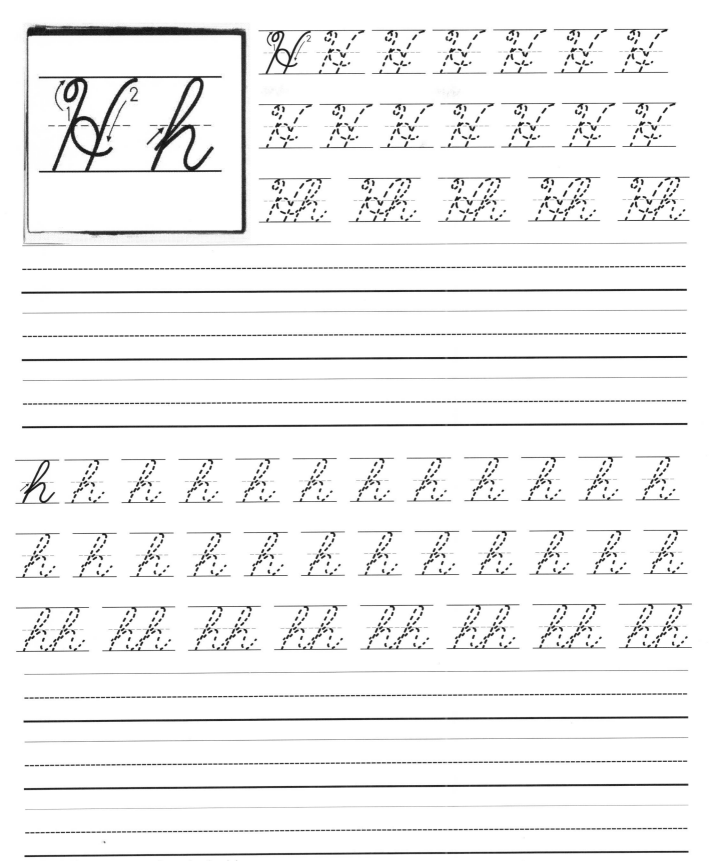

Circle your best letter

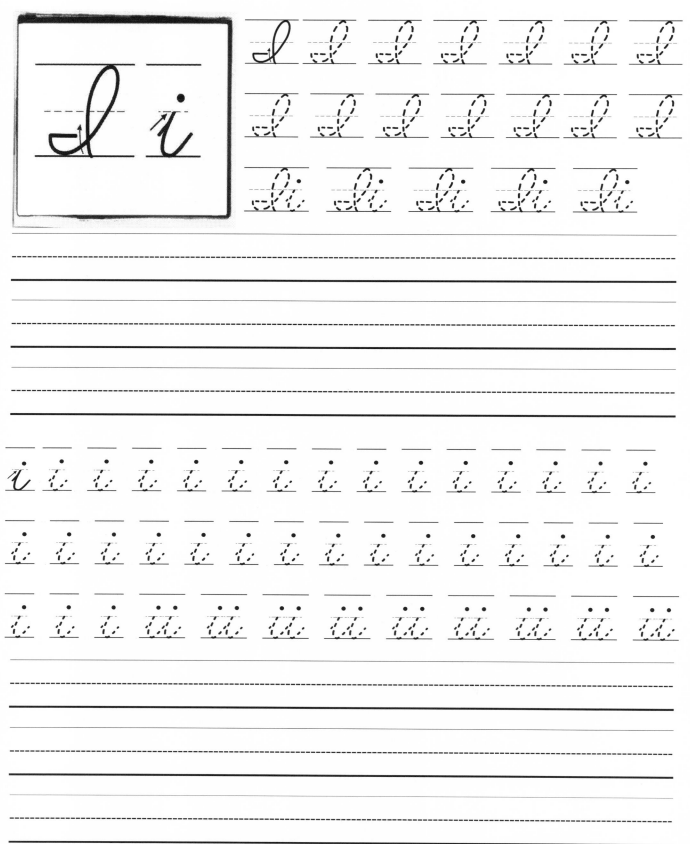

Circle your best letter

Circle your best letter

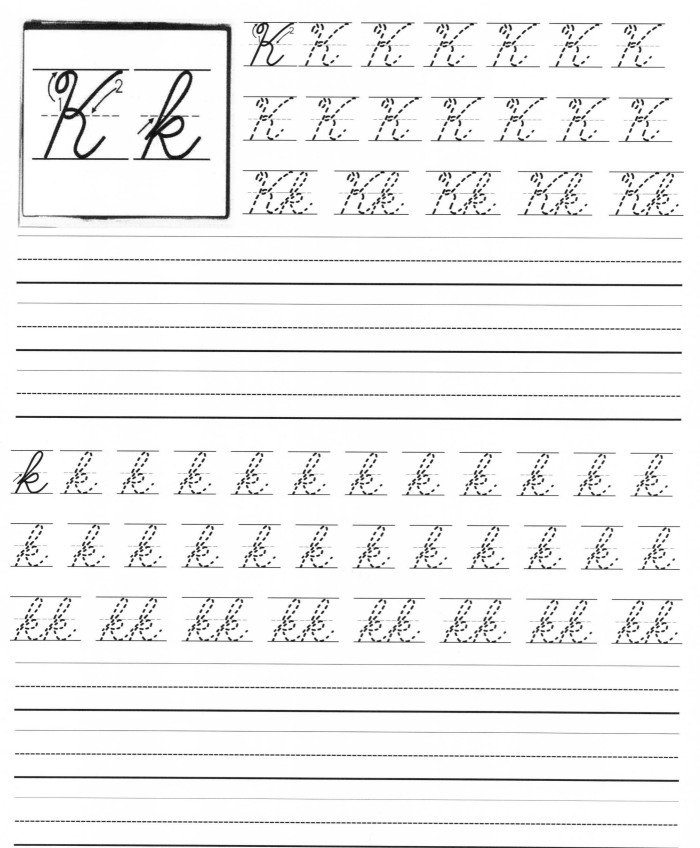

Circle your best letter

Circle your best letter

M m

M M M M M M M M M M M M M Mm Mm

m m m m m m m m m
m m m m m m m m m
mm mm mm mm mm

Circle your best letter

$\mathcal{N} \ n$

$\mathcal{N} \ \mathcal{N} \ \mathcal{N} \ \mathcal{N} \ \mathcal{N} \ \mathcal{N} \ \mathcal{N}$

$\mathcal{N} \ \mathcal{N} \ \mathcal{N} \ \mathcal{N} \ \mathcal{N} \ \mathcal{N} \ \mathcal{N}$

$\mathcal{N}n \ \mathcal{N}n \ \mathcal{N}n \ \mathcal{N}n$

$n \ n \ n \ n \ n \ n \ n \ n \ n \ n$

$n \ n \ n \ n \ n \ n \ n \ n \ n \ n$

$nn \ nn \ nn \ nn \ nn \ nn$

Circle your best letter

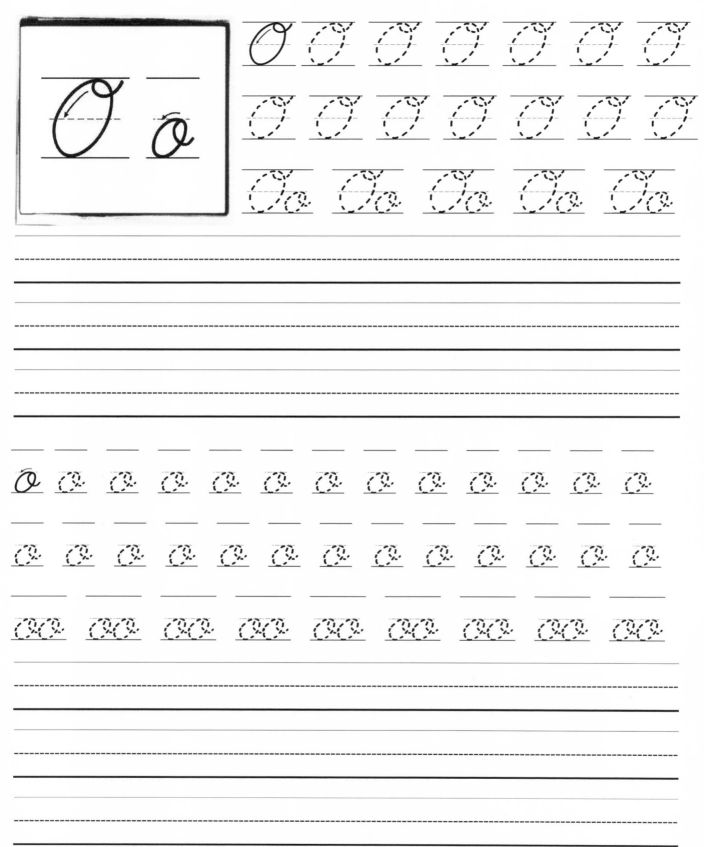

Circle your best letter

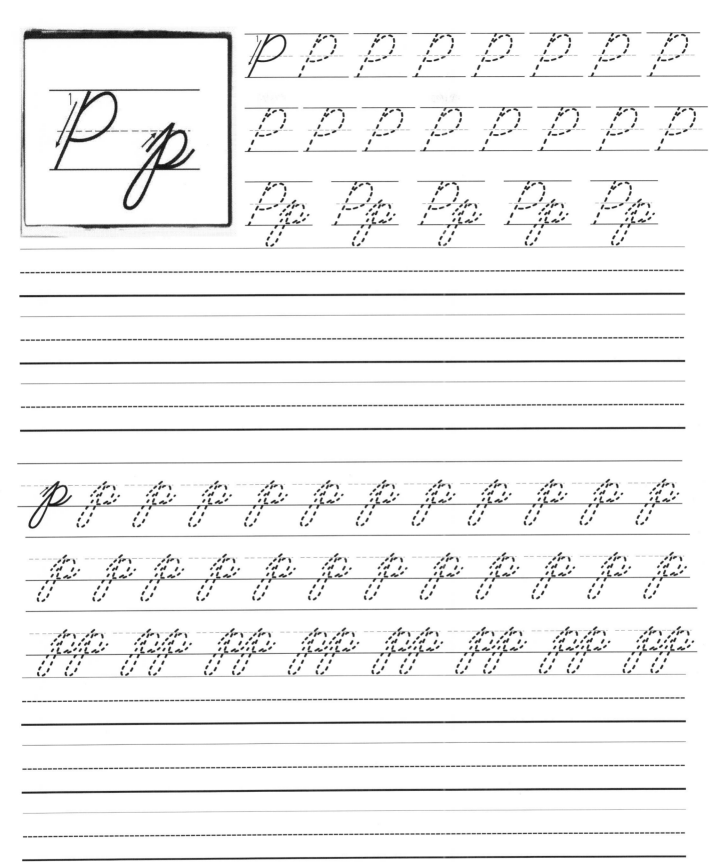

Circle your best letter

2 q

2 2 2 2 2 2 2
2 2 2 2 2 2 2
2q 2q 2q 2q 2q

q q q q q q q q q q q q
q q q q q q q q q q q q
qq qq qq qq qq qq qq qq qq

Circle your best letter

R r

R R R R R R R
R R R R R R R
Rr Rr Rr Rr Rr

n n n n n n n n n n n n n n
n n n n n n n n n n n n n n
nn nn nn nn nn nn nn nn nn

Circle your best letter

Circle your best letter

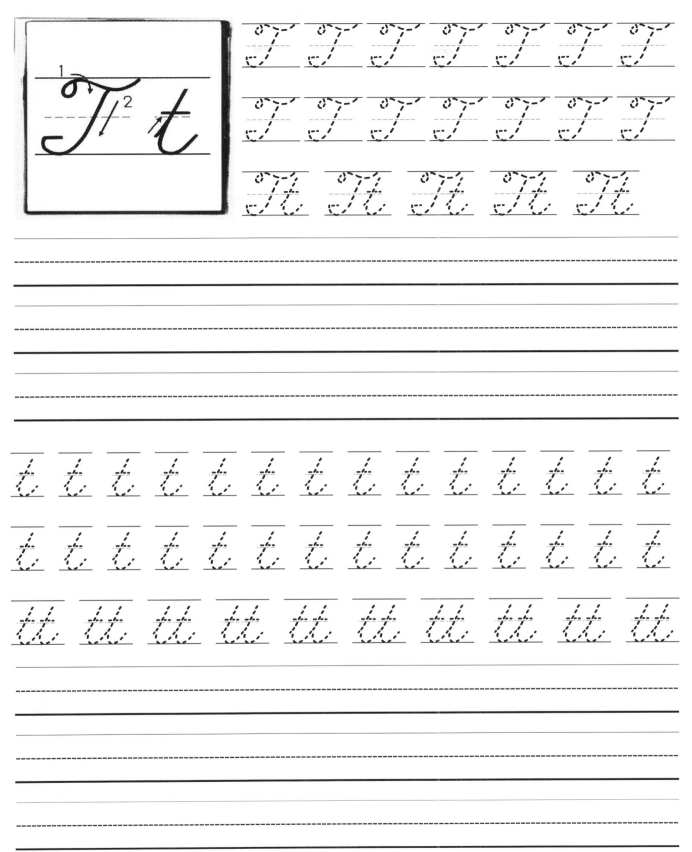

Circle your best letter

$\mathcal{U}$ u

$\mathcal{U}$ $\mathcal{U}$ $\mathcal{U}$ $\mathcal{U}$ $\mathcal{U}$ $\mathcal{U}$ $\mathcal{U}$

$\mathcal{U}$ $\mathcal{U}$ $\mathcal{U}$ $\mathcal{U}$ $\mathcal{U}$ $\mathcal{U}$ $\mathcal{U}$

$\mathcal{U}u$ $\mathcal{U}u$ $\mathcal{U}u$ $\mathcal{U}u$

u u u u u u u u u u

u u u u u u u u u u

uu uu uu uu uu uu uu

Circle your best letter

U u

U U U U U U U U
U U U U U U U
Uu Uu Uu Uu

u u u u u u u u u u u
u u u u u u u u u u u
uu uu uu uu uu uu uu

Circle your best letter

U u

Uu Uu Uu Uu Uu
Uu Uu Uu Uu Uu
Uw Uw Uw

uw uw uw uw uw uw uw uw uw uw
uw uw uw uw uw uw uw uw uw uw
uwuw uwuw uwuw uwuw uwuw uwuw

Circle your best letter

Circle your best letter

Circle your best letter

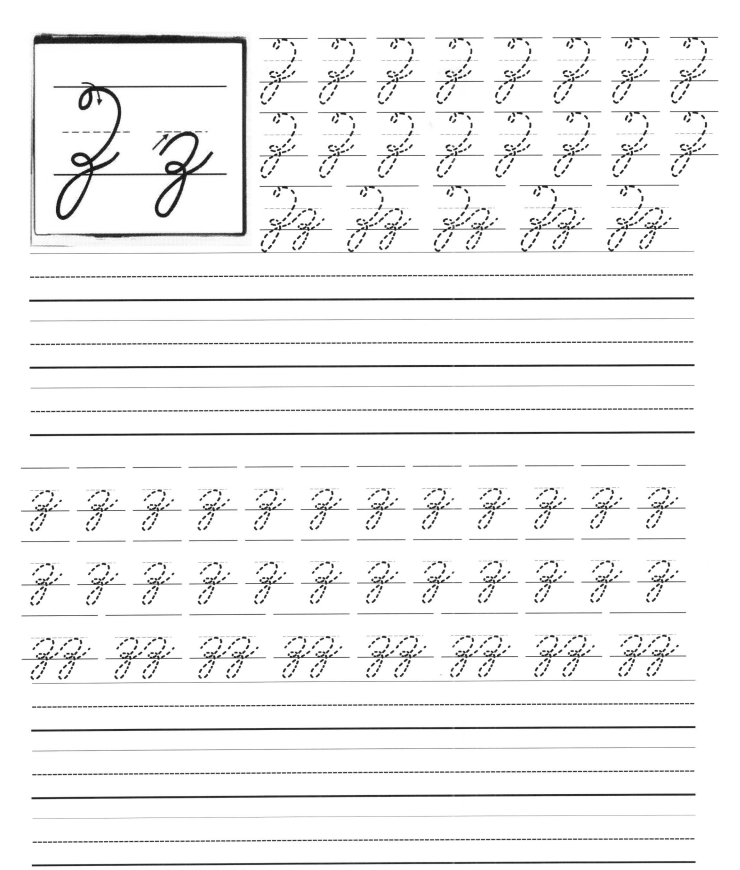

Circle your best letter

Part Two: Word Practice

- Copy two to three pages a week.

- First trace over every letter, then copy words onto blank rows.

- Check your child's work to correct any bad habits or confusion.

- Have your child circle their best word on the workbook page to help train their eyes as well as their hand.

Aslan Aslan Aslan

Bree Bree Bree

Caspian Caspian Caspian

dragon dragon dragon

Edmund Edmund Edmund

faun faun faun

giant *giant* *giant*

horse *horse* *horse*

island *island* *island*

Jill Jill Jill

Kirke Kirke Kirke

lion lion lion

mouse mouse mouse

Narnia Narnia Narnia

owls owls owls

Peter Peter Peter

queen queen queen

Reepicheep Reepicheep Reepicheep

Susan Susan Susan

Tumnus Tumnus Tumnus

Eustace Eustace Eustace

voyage *voyage* *voyage*

wolf *wolf* *wolf*

fox *fox* *fox*

Lucy Lucy Lucy

Puzzle Puzzle Puzzle

Part Three:
Quote Copywork

- Copy one to three quotes a week, depending on your childs ability.

- The quotes get longer and progressively harder, so depending on your child's pace, they may need to take a few days to finish the longer quote. Keep it fun!

- Check your child's work to correct any bad habits or confusion.

- For a fun challenge, try to find the quotes and read the context.

"Courage, dear heart."

—Voyage of the Dawn Treader

"Aslan is on the move."

−The Lion, the Witch, and the Wardrobe

"Things never happen the same way twice dear one."

–Prince Caspian

"Let us go and take the adventure that shall fall to us."

—The Lion, the Witch, and the Wardrobe

"Here is your brother," he said, "and there is no need to talk to him about what has passed."

—The Lion, the Witch, and the Wardrobe.

*"By knowing me here for a little,
you will know me better there."*

−Voyage of the Dawn Treader

"Adventures are never fun while you're having them."

–Voyage of the Dawn Treader

"Whatever we do, don't let's have any running. Especially not before supper; and not too soon after it neither."

–Prince Caspian

"Child," said the Voice, "I am telling your story, not hers. I tell no one any story but his own."

–A Horse and His Boy

"You would not have called to me unless I had been calling you."

−The Silver Chair

"It is very true. But even a traitor may mend. I have known one who did."

−A Horse and His Boy

"All shall be done, but it may be harder than you think."

—The Lion, The Witch, and the Wardrobe

"All get what they want; they do not always like it."

-The Magician's Nephew

"One always feels better when one has made up one's mind."

—The Last Battle

"Peter did not feel very brave; indeed, he felt he was going to be sick. But that made no difference to what he had to do."

–The Lion, the Witch, and the Wardrobe

"Girls aren't very good at keeping maps in their brains", said Edmund. "That's because we've got something in them", replied Lucy.

—Prince Caspian

"Now the trouble about trying to make yourself stupider than you really are is that you very often succeed."

—The Magician's Nephew

"For what you see and hear depends a good deal on where you are standing: it also depends on what sort of person you are."

—The Magician's Nephew

"See the Bear in his own den
before you judge of his conditions."
–Horse and His Boy

"Have patience, like us beasts. The help will come. It may be even now at the door."

—Prince Caspian

"No great wisdom can be reached without sacrifice."

—The Magician's Nephew

"You doubt your value. Don't run from who you are."

–Prince Caspian

"Child," said Aslan, "did I not explain
to you once before that no one is ever
told what would have happened?"

–Voyage of the Dawn Treader

"The king's under the law, for it's the law makes him a king."

—A Horse and His Boy

"It's rather late to be thinking of precautions now there we're inside and the door is shut behind us."

—The Silver Chair

"This is the land I have been looking for all my life, though I never knew it till now."

—The Last Battle

"Every year you grow, you will find me bigger."

—Prince Caspian

"Lucy woke out of the deepest sleep you can imagine, with the feeling that the voice she liked best in the world had been calling her name."

–Prince Caspian

"Who said anything about safe? 'Course he isn't safe. But he's good. He's the King, I tell you."

—The Lion, The Witch, and the Wardrobe

"In our world too, a stable once had something inside it that was bigger than our whole world."

—The Last Battle

"Courage, child: we are all between the paws of the true Aslan."

—The Last Battle

ABOUT THE AUTHOR

Robyn Joyner has always loved children's literature and teaching.
She has a degree in Early Childhood and is currently is a homeschool mother and writer.
She lives in Northern Indiana with her husband and twin sons.

Find more books at www.LearningCursive.org

Homeschool Blog at www.LeadingThemToTheRock.com

Facebook- @totherockhomeschool

Learning Cursive in Narnia is part of Learning Cursive Series by Robyn Joyner

First Published Edition: June 2019

Independently published via Kindle Direct Publishing

ISBN-10 : 1072561085

ISBN-13 : 978-1072561088

Cover Illustrations & Curriculum Formatting © 2019 Robyn Joyner

Quotes from *The Complete Chronicles of Narnia* © 1956 C.S. Lewis

Find more books at www.LearningCursive.org

Made in the USA
Las Vegas, NV
13 March 2024